FREE HUGS

Grateful acknowledgment is made to the following publications in which some of these poems first appeared, often in slightly different versions: *Coastal Shelf, Cream City Review, Cutthroat Journal, Four Chambers, Kentucky Review, Lockdown Prayers, Open Arts Forum, RATTLE,* and *Whitefish Review.*

Some of these poems also appeared in:

Get Serious (Tucson, Arizona: Chax Press, 2013), chosen a Southwest Best Book of 2013 by the Tucson/Pima County Library

Diphtheria Festival (Charlotte, North Carolina: Main Street Rag Publishing Co., 2016)

Birkenstock Blues (Rockford, Michigan: Presa Press, 2019)

Yesternow (Philadelphia, PA: Moonstone Press, 2023)

Also by Jefferson Carter

Taking Chances   (Desert First Works, 1976)
Gentling the Horses   (Maguey Press, 1979)
None of This Will Kill Me   (Moon Pony Press, 1987)
Tough Love   (Riverstone Press, 1993)
Homemade Arrows   (Red Felt Publishing, 2000)
Litter Box   (Spork Press, 2004)
Sentimemtal Blue   (Chax Press, 2007)
My Kind of Animal   (Chax Press, 2010)
Get Serious: New and Selected Poems   (Chax Press, 2013)
Diptheria Festival   (Main Street Rag Publishing Co., 2016)
Birkenstock Blues   (Presa Press, 2019)
Yesternow   (Moonstone Press, 2023)

Free Hugs
Selected and New Poems

Jefferson Carter

Free Hugs: Selected and New Poems. Copyright © 2025 Jefferson Carter

Cover painting: *Rincon #2* © 1984 by Jim Waid. Acrylic on canvas, 60" x 72". Used by permission.

Author photograph: Bill Moeller

Cover and book design: Jordan Jones

All rights reserved. No part of this publication may be reproduced, stored in a retrieval system or transmitted in any form or by any means, electronic, mechanical, photocopying, recording or otherwise without the prior permission of the publisher.

Library of Congress Control Number: 2024951586

ISBN Paper 978-1-58775-058-8
      E-Book 978-1-58775-059-5

1 3 5 7 9 10 8 6 4 2

Coyote Arts LLC
PO Box 6690
Albuquerque, New Mexico 87197-6690
www.coyote-arts.com

for my family: Connie, Evan, Cristina, Maria, and Mila

Contents

from *Get Serious*

Mockingbird	3
American Ingenuity	4
Kill Data	5
Don't Tell	6
Arbitrary	7
Blame Sutra	8
Pasture	9
Sunlight	10
Mall	11
King Onela's Dog	12
Memento Mori	14
Amulet	15
Cat Pose	16

from *Diphtheria Festival*

Walk (This Way)	19
Genealogy	20
Tsunami	21
Spirit Animal	22
The Note I Left	23
Heavy	24
Stardust	25
Postal Sonnet	26
Ear	27
The Falling Man	28

from *Birkenstock Blues*

Life Partner	31
Segue	32
Guyz Night Out	33
The Judgment-Free Zone	34
Thump	35
Ode to My Soft Palate	36
Cat & Snake	37
Cat & Transient	38
Cat & Apocalypse I	39
The Book of Extinctions	40
The Last Bumper Sticker	41
Sticker	42
For My Sister, The Feminist	44
Danger Ranger	45

from *Yesternow*

Southern Fried	49
Cashmere	50
Blog Not	52
Walden (Do as I Say, Not as I Do)	54
Sonoita	55
Indelible	56
Thin Skin	57
Fuzzy Tree	58
Shotgun	59
Boomer	61
The Grilling Dead	62
Plague Mask	64

New Poems

Here Comes the Sun	67
Yesternow	68
Hav-A-Hart	70
White Giant	72
Cat & Apocalypse II	74
Family Values	75
The Last Generation	76
The Spirit Animal Society	78
Viejo	79
Help! I've Fallen….	80
80 Is the New 50	81
Hermit	82
Microwave	83
Business as Usual	85
Body Poetry	86
American Chestnut	87
Kufi	88
Sugar, Sugar	89
What Is Porn?	90
The Pope	91
High Hopes	93
They Told Me to Interrogate My White Male Cishet Privilege	94
Meditating	95

from *Get Serious*

Mockingbird

Our third president owned
a pet mockingbird named Dick.
Let's not mention what else
he owned. Dick dug Monticello,
that big white layer cake.
He'd click & chatter. He'd mimic
the field slaves' hosannahs
until he'd almost faint, wobbling
on his perch like a double
fistful of dirty cotton.

American Ingenuity

After a buffalo burger
& some butter lettuce,
triple-washed, I'm ready
to refinance the house.
I can't sleep nights,
coveting the sudden wealth
of someone like Ragged Dick
the bootblack, a fictional
character, but still....

I'd vote Socialist. I can't sleep,
concocting get-rich-quick schemes:
a great-tasting colonoscopy prep.
Or *Hasta* Yoga, copywriting,
like Mr. Bikram, ancient asanas,
the ones that stretch wrist & fingers,
yoga for signatories. I'd vote
Socialist. My best idea yet,
lavender-scented formaldehyde.

Kill Data

My soap, cruelty-free,
hand-crafted, contains
olive oil. I smell

like a salad. Do Muslim
men do household chores?
I consider converting.

Did their ancestors, like
ours, keep kill data?

"After mass, December 23,
1940, Santa Cruz River,
a jaguar, male, roped,
killed with rocks, 138 lbs,
tail 72 inches, stomach
full of frogs." Can you
even say this is in Arabic?

from Get Serious

Don't Tell

I heard Mick Jagger's got
a small penis. I heard Anne Waldman
recite her 900-page feminist epic,
The Iovis Trilogy. A friend suggested
a lapel pin, a crown of thorns, for anyone
who finishes it. I bought a copy,
glued the middle pages, then cut out
a hiding place for my new 9 mm.
Don't tell. I'm off to the moisture farm.
I registered for a workshop
titled "Shuffling Off This Moral Coil,"
where I'll confess to thoughts like
"You be the dancer, I'll be the pole."

Arbitrary

I'm biking across campus,
wondering why two nipples?
Why not one like a whale
or eight like a dog? Why
two legs, walking upright?
Wouldn't we be happier
on all fours? No more
middle-aged back troubles
& we'd move at that slower pace
the gurus recommend.
We'd be kinder, balancing
on two knees and one hand
at an intersection, gesturing
to our fellow quadrupeds, "no,
please, you go first." It could
happen. Everything's so
arbitrary. I could snarl
at that coed jogging
in the bike lane, "Don't give me
the stink eye!" I could even tell her
someday you'll feel like me,
like a barely legal alien
on a stolen unicycle. Or not.

Blame Sutra

I blame yoga, no, not yoga, I blame
Buddhism. In Sanskrit, "modesty"
means not calling attention to yourself.
In American, "poetry" means calling
attention to yourself. When I perform
(or "preform," as the racing program
misspells it, "see the Budweiser Clydesdales
preform"), when I perform my poems,
I want to clap a hand over my mouth.
Shut the fuck up & let someone else talk!
Those ghosts & mannequins around you,
they all have a tale to tell. If you listen,
you'll hear the breath that breathes us all.
Don't & you'll tell jokes like this: in Texas,
foreplay means asking "you awake?"

Pasture

To a narcissist, all
the world's a mirror.
The day I misread
the no trespassing sign
in the laundromat window
as no trepanning, I retired
from narcissism. I stopped
worrying about my headaches.
I'm not so lonely now
& even a goat isn't just
a goat. I told my neighbor
my lawn's a pasture & today
I saw a herd, fainting goats
he calls them, grazing there.

Sunlight

I remember lying
on Nancy's bed,
Nancy on one side,
her older sister
on the other, sunlight
warming our bare legs
as I recited my new poem
& I remember thinking
I love women, the way
they smell, how they look
& feel, the nightclub
of my mind quiet for once,
the poem describing
a sentient rock, a hermit
who sealed up the entrance
to his cave, leaving a slit
through which the villagers
pushed his food.

Mall

All those air-brushed models,
12-feet-tall, pouting & whispering,
"I'm beautiful. You're not."
I forgive my internal (I wanted
to say eternal) erection. We're
hard-wired to respond to beauty.
I don't forgive Victoria's Secret,
those poor teenage girls flip, flip,
flipping their straightened hair
or plucking at their skinny jeans,
plumbers' cracks & camel toes,
or giving this old man dirty looks
as if there's a thought balloon
over my head. I'm not being
flippant. What if love means never
having to say you're beautiful?

King Onela's Dog

The Beowulf poet sang
about "A balm in bed
to the battle-scarred Swede."
Some scholar translated
"balm in bed" as "sleeping
companion," identifying
this companion as King Onela's
favorite dog, not his queen,
but you know scholars, anything
to get published. A dog's nose
is 100 times more sensitive
than a man's. The Great Hall,
unwashed bodies, animal skins,
chamber pots under the table,
guests, gorged, vomiting
onto the floor, ready for the
next course. To be a dog then
must have been very heaven!
Around 400 A.D. these dogs
got together & swore fealty to man,
to be his disco ball & best friend
forever. What did the dogs

get in return? All you can
eat, some glorious stinks & best
of all, the infinite loneliness
of the two-legged tribes.

Memento Mori

My wife's the best-looking person
at this party. I'm second-best.
Someone's bald mother slumps
in her wheelchair, surprised to be
a memento mori. Their arthritic feet
like satyrs' hooves, others keep
losing their flip-flops as they do
the mash-potato & sing "Do
You Love Me?" We don't need no
stinking paranormal urban fantasies,
but doesn't anyone want to leave
a good-looking corpse anymore?

All the poets my age are now
writing about death. No more
heavy-breathing, no more sexual healing
or swooning at life's infinite possibilities.
"Death," wrote the poet, "be not proud."
I'd like to add, "At least be stylish
or try to smell nice." Don't feel bad.
It's not you. It's the formaldehyde.

Amulet

The vet calls it "extrusion" & prescribes
an antibiotic, room-temperature, as if the cat
cares. He'll lose that fang in a few weeks.
I ask the vet if she knows some place
that could gold-plate the tooth & hang it
on a silver chain, an amulet against
this evil century. She shrugs & glances
away as if I'm a Scientologist or mentally ill.
O, ye of little faith!! The Mai Mai rebels
believed holy water changed the bullets
of the government troops into rain.
They brandished spears, wearing nothing
but shower caps on their heads & around
their necks, bath plugs for amulets.
Easy pose not easy no more. Nothing not
easy no more. But come, hang this cat's tooth
around your neck & see how much it helps.
The Mai Mai rebels? 20% almost survived.

Cat Pose

My mat smells
like cat chow.
As that old song
"Somebody's Watching You"
doesn't say, nobody's
watching you.
Both cats nap on the chair
below the cooler vent
& I return to my breath,
preparing for corpse pose.
My teacher likes
"hospice" as a metaphor
for life. We're all patients.
Why maim each other?

from *Diphtheria Festival*

Walk (This Way)

Soon to be a major motion picture,
Shirley MacLaine's spiritual journey,
her pilgrimage to Santiago de Compostela.
St. James, the brother of Jesus,
penned the bestseller *My Brother
Was an Only Child.* His martyred
& flensed corpse sailed in a stone boat
from Jerusalem, guided by angels
across the Mediterranean to Galicia,
where his bones now rest. *Peregrino,*
I've got some carbon anti-shock
trekking poles to sell you, some
blister-proof virgin wool socks. I've got
a sharp black sunhat emblazoned
with the Walk This Way yellow arrow
& I've got a self-fulfilling water bottle.
Peregrino, are you lost? I've got a butterfly
to sell you, a butterfly disguised as a soul
& trained to follow you for miles.

Genealogy

The Old Testament says
his testicles were like unto
a donkey's, swollen gray
pomegranates, his emissions
like unto a river in full spate.

My ancestor? Yours? No,
don't google biblicalmoneyshots.com.
He's a lie, a lie invented
by a dry prophet. But as any pastor
worth his salt won't tell you, it's
not a lie if you believe it.

Tsunami

I've been thinking lately about tsunamis,
dreaming about them. We're at the beach,
working on our skin cancer, when the horizon
starts trembling. I wake up, wondering
why I can't visualize the approaching wave,
its height or velocity, its changing colors.
I don't mean stock images from disaster movies,
the familiar magic of CGI, a cruise ship
swanning past, big as a city block, a wave
tossing her like a piece of driftwood.
Someone once told me what you
can't imagine can't happen—
the shadow of the approaching wave
rising against the buildings like night filling
up the window when you raise the shade.

Spirit Animal

My animal? The platypus,
of course. Not the penguin,
too black & white. Not the wolverine,
ferocious & smelly. The horse?
No, why share with all those
white women who call themselves
Nightwind? The platypus reminds
me of me, his ambivalence,
his moral versatility, his head
like a furry spatula. Did you know
the platypus boasts a poisonous spur
on each thigh? Nerve damage,
paralysis, death. His spirit
animal? Me, of course.

The Note I Left

I dreamed about Cher, not
about Sonny. I dreamed about. . .
whatever. I always dream & learn
nothing, Freud notwithstanding.

I'm awake now, our cat
butting my legs, the furniture,
all four walls. Does he know
I'm leaving? I pick him up

& kiss him between the ears,
goodbye. Someone said sentimentality
is the poor man's poetry. The note
I left for you? A rich man's prose.

Heavy

When in bed she throws her thigh
across mine, I recall that old slogan,
"He ain't heavy. He's my brother."

She ain't heavy. She's my wife.
But she is heavy. When I shift her head
because she's snoring, it's heavy
as a kettlebell. Awake, what's
heavier than her cheerful gravitas,
which the online dictionary points out
rhymes with "forward pass." When we leave

a party, friends say to each other, "She's
a saint, his wife. He can be such
an asshole!" Who knows what a soul
weighs? A ton of feathers or a ton
of lead, I know what love can weigh.

Stardust

> "We are stardust. We are golden."
> — Joni Mitchell

We talk for hours about having
nothing to talk about.

After all these years, we still
don't resemble each other.

To entertain her, I wonder
out loud about eating the cat.
Would his thigh taste like dark meat?

Rushing to get ready, she asks
"What is wrong with you?"

Stardust? No, more like
radon & neon, those noble gases

which don't bond but boil
separately at the same temperature.

Postal Sonnet

Today's mail: an invitation to join
Arizona's liveliest burial society.
Another illegible, handwritten note
offering to landscape the front yard.

A letter from my shrink informing me he's
closing his practice. He extends best wishes
for my future health & happiness.
I don't panic. I suppose I'm cured.

I'll miss our sessions, discussing poetry
& joking about a better life through chemistry.
Now who will answer my inconsequential
questions, the ones nobody else cares about?

Did you know in Eastern psychology,
the word "personality" means scar tissue?

Ear

You want a Jesuit to help stop
your suffering, someone smarter
than you. But isn't that the problem?

So what if your third wife bought
a bottle of perfume called Shake It,
Shake It, Señora? Let those
middle-aged ladies shake their
money makers. Let the world

shake itself into its recurring patterns
of class conflict, raging heterosexuality
& unsanctioned acts of milky kindness.

Her therapist told my friend all
she needed was a wall to talk to,
a wall composed of ears. You want a Jesuit,
but once you accept any ear will do,
any ear will do. I'm listening.

The Falling Man

The tower's gray & white stripes
like a corduroy curtain behind him,
the man, dark-skinned, wearing
a pale sports coat & black slacks,
the man isn't falling. I've superglued
the photo upside-down to the inside
of my closet door. He isn't falling,
one knee lifted, arms rigid, trapping
the billowing skirts of his jacket
against his sides. He's anyone
I can imagine. The father of many girls.
An expert on the language of Greenland,
which has no expletives. A novice step dancer
practicing his routine. Sometimes, when
no one's around, I open the closet door
& say, "Good morning, Dancing Man."

from *Birkenstock Blues*

Life Partner

For convenience, I & my life partner
(the woman formerly known as my wife)
have numbered our arguments. Number 3,
you're so negative. Number 8, you're
naive. Number 11, another beer already?
Number 13, you don't listen to me.

But I do. I just don't agree. Now
my life partner's on the couch, watching
Live P.D. She's pleased with the police,
so kind to the miscreants & trailer trash
they apprehend. Of course, they're
kind! They're on camera! Without
looking at me, she holds up three fingers.

My life partner wants to make a deal:
she'll stop storing our broken pepper mill
upright in the spice rack, pepper everywhere
like coarse soot, she'll store the mill
on its side if I stop switching off the light
over the dining-room table whenever
she's in another room. Why? Why
does she need that light on all day?
She raises both fists & opens each one
twice. Number 20, you don't love me.

Segue

When the band segues from "Cupid"
to "Chain Gang," I stop dancing.
My hip hurts & I feel foolish, doing
the two-step to "Hoh! Ah! Hoh! Ah,"
the sound of the men working
on the chain gang. You keep dancing,
raising an imaginary pick ax over your head
on each "Hoh!" & striking on each "Ah!"
Love, for a shy girl, you don't sweat
much, meaning I love how you don't sweat
being judged. I sit down to my bottle
of flat beer, dreading tonight, knowing
I'll get up between nightmares six
or seven times to pee. Here comes
"Mustang Sally" & I slice a forefinger
across my throat, which means
"I'm dead, love. Let's go home."

Guyz Night Out

My friend told me
he's got to move, the space
rent-free but the ceiling
so low, he bumps his head
when he's having sex or even
when he's making love.

Much younger than I
(or me, as educated Brits say),
he's old enough to make such
fine distinctions. I joked,
"Rent-free? When I was
your age, I would've died
for a coffin, rent-free."

Two happy drunks, we
discussed interspecies dating
& our issues with intimacy.

Right now, my wife's glaring at me
from the couch. I'm worried
she wasn't grateful to the
cops who drove me home.

The Judgment-Free Zone

You've entered the judgment-free zone.
Speaking of entering (or never entering
anything ever again), here's a flyer
for clothing-optional yoga....

Imagine the enthusiastically naked yogi
in front of you, clasping his / her / their big toes
during *Prasarita Padottanasana*
(Wide-legged Forward Bend).

My long-dead musician friend sang,
"There's gotta be a limit!" How I miss him.

Thump

His burnt-orange t-shirt,
black letters above the image
of an AR-15, the slogan:
"quickest way to a man's heart."
I'd describe him, but why bother?

My shrink left town,
so I'll ask myself myself, how
did that make you feel,
that T-shirt? How? Like

the other night when a sound
woke me, not the thumpety-thump,
thumpety-thump of the cats playing
but the thump-scrape, thump-scrape
of something dragging itself
down the hall to my bedroom.

Like that.

Ode to My Soft Palate

I love my soft palate,
flexible, adroit, which, when sucking
or swallowing, rises, creating
a vacuum in my oral cavity,
which keeps food
out of my respiratory tract.
In other words,
I can eat without inhaling
into my lungs chunks
of my organic jackfruit
or humanely-raised Barramundi.

Also, I love my uvula,
that fleshy, elongated projection
that terminates my soft palate,
its seromucous glands
& excretory canals
lubricating my mouth
so I can pronounce certain
consonants essential to a language
like Arabic, which, according
to our neighbors, Mr. & Mrs.
MAGA & their septic
yard signs, will soon become
our national tongue.

Cat & Snake

I swore I'd stop writing
about cats. But here she comes
down the hall, our little black cat,
retrieving the catnip caterpillar for me
to throw again. Even a silly movie
like *Escape from L.A.* addresses
more consequential subjects. When
Snake pushes the button that destroys
the global power grid forever, when he
lights that forbidden American Spirit cigarette
& blows out the match, we're inflamed:
"Fuck it! Let's just start all over again!"
Until then, I'm sitting here cross-legged
on the floor, a cat squirming in my lap,
staring up at me like a startled owl,
her body dense as a bean bag. Ok.
The only subjects worth writing about
are love & death but consider this:
if I died in the house, you know what the cat
would do after three days without food.

Cat & Transient

The homeless guy who lowers himself
down beside me on the bench
outside the Co-op? He's generic,
more dirt than human, his stink
killing my appetite for the bowl
of organic jackfruit on my lap. I stand,
ashamed, give him a dollar & walk away
after dumping the paper bowl
into a trashcan advertising the pleasures
of our historic shopping district.

I swore I'd stop writing about liberal guilt
& about cats too, but I must confess
last night, I groomed our little black cat
with my tongue & watched her perpetually
startled gold eyes widen as I licked her neck
& then her belly, inhaling her scent.
In Japan, childless couples can rent
a cat by the hour to sniff its belly, which
smells like the crown of a baby's head.

Cat & Apocalypse I

I'm watching our little black cat
sitting in the sink, drinking
from the faucet, her eyes closed
in ecstasy. When the world ends,
I won't mourn my fucked-up species.
I'll regret our cat's moment of terror
when the water turns to flame.

The Book of Extinctions

You already know about
the ivory-billed woodpecker
& the passenger pigeon,
but how about Gilbert's potoroo
or the Martinique pilori?
Goodbye, freckled dibbler.
Goodbye, barred bandicoot.

Extinct Species of the World,
published in 1990, calculates
that "more than 100 species
a day will have disappeared by the end
of the century." The publishers
now want an editor to revise
& update the book, some dry-eyed
expert at saying goodbye.

The Last Bumper Sticker

Do you believe in magic?
Sorry. I meant science.
Geospatially-stratified
random sampling? Field
specific conductance?
How about spheres of discharge,
multiple seeping sources,
climate refugia? No?

Then adjust your earbuds.
Get ready for some extreme
karst, for guest ethicists & your
favorite Boko Haram musicals.

"Adam had 'em," the first poem
about fleas. The first joke
about rabbits: "It'll be fun,
wasn't it?" The last bumper sticker:
"No jobs on a dead planet."

Sticker

Now, "they" say
our prehistoric ancestors
didn't go to bed at sundown
but hung around the campfire
for hours. Doing what?
I can't imagine. I myself
one night got so bored,
I slept with a woman
who looked like John Denver.

Seriously though, imagine
yourself, beetle-browed,
prognathic, stinking of caribou fat,
the sun down & the darkness
lit by fireflies big as lanterns,
some guttural rendition
of "Kumbaya" rising in your throat.

Did you imagine the future,
your enemies on a spit, winds
hammering pieces of straw
like nails into a tree trunk,
something brighter than the sun

boiling the lake below?
Or did you imagine a sticker
on your war club, exhorting you
& your sleepy tribesmen to be kind?

For My Sister, The Feminist

You told me
I can't imagine
what it's like
being a woman.

But I can imagine
being a spoon, a loaf
of bread, a hummingbird,
even a werewolf,
in-grown hairs & all.
Why not a woman?

Don't you remember
the night you woke up
sobbing & I left
my bed down the hall
to hold your hand
until you fell back to sleep?

Danger Ranger

Last night's curry for breakfast,
eating with my hands as I drive,
Miles on the radio & I'm thinking
about a myth, a bird born without feet,
its wingspan wide as a man's, doomed
never to land & sleep....

The National Forest Service wants
a Danger Ranger, someone who
doesn't sleep, a volunteer to update
Fire Danger Today signs, to move every
arrow on every sign as the weather
changes....

Love, after you've gone, I'll volunteer
for the job, a Danger Ranger updating
the signs as the weather changes,
never sleeping again....

from *Yesternow*

Southern Fried

Excuse me, you're standing
on my tongue. I do love
your philtrum, by the way,
how it separates your nose
from your upper lip.

You can't eat a fertilized egg
in Alabama. Preborn chickens
have rights there. Postborn
chickens, however, may be
baked or southern fried.
Food for thought.

Answer this: are you
better off now than you were
thirty seconds ago? I know,
I know, funny as a barrel
of hazardous waste.

But loving you? Like
speed-dating a cobra.

Cashmere

When my mother was 77,
she fell in love again.
She invited the object of her affections,
an elderly man she met in church,
to a party at my big sister's home.

He arrived with another man, both
wearing identical powder-blue
cashmere sweaters. My sister,
whose gaydar is sensitive as a
geiger counter, raised her eyebrows at me.
I shrugged back. Now, dear reader,

don't expect me to mention
toxic masculinity, how my father,
modeling a man's proper relationship
to nature, forced my six-year-old son to shoot
a desert cottontail with a pellet gun,
how my father brooded for three days
in a darkened room because someone
told him I was a homosexual. No, no

expectations, yours or those of my
widowed mother as she flirted,
innocent as a zygote, trying to

hold hands with this diffident man
who, beneath the kitchen counter,
pressed his leg against the leg
of the one he came with.

Blog Not

I won't blog.
Don't ask me. I've got
nothing to say.
Except this: a rising tide
lifts all yachts or
no jobs on a dead planet.
See? Nothing
but ineffectual liberal aphorisms.

Someday
anybody can say anything.
I'd blog about Scooter,
my old gelding, who'd get a boner
while biting our mare's ass.
"Look!" shrieked my sister.
"It's pink and black!"

Or I'd gossip
about famous poets, the one
who snorts like a rhinoceros
when he reads & the one
who revised his anthologized poem,
changing the line "we must
love one another or die" to

"we must love one another
& die." Speaking of love & death,
the only subjects worth writing about,
I've got nothing to say.

Except this:
against his cardiologist's orders,
my father made love to my mother.
Minutes later, she found
him on the bathroom floor,
dead. And yes, lying there,
slumped against the bathtub,
yes, he was smiling.

Walden (Do as I Say, Not as I Do)

Most evenings, Thoreau would stroll
the two miles to his mother's house,
where he'd enjoy a nice, home-cooked meal.

Does this mean the mass of men
don't lead lives of quiet desperation?
That you shouldn't simplify your life?

Not at all. Don't forget our most moral
Moral Philosophers admonished us
in Latin, *Fac quod dico, non quod facio*

while Thoreau himself endorsed
Rhodiola Rosea, an adaptogenic herb
that reduces cynicism 40 percent
in all but the most severe cases.

Sonoita

How to depict
these yellow hills,
the datura, chalk white
along the road?

First person singular, that
point-of-view impugned
by literary theorists? What
about foregrounding?
Signifier or signified?

Look! Metal silhouettes
of a working man on a horse
herding a cow & her calf
home along the ridge.

Indelible

I blended five bananas
& some unsweetened coconut milk
to create that contradiction in terms,
"a healthful dessert." In the words
of a former friend, who wanted
to be a poet, "this shit's indelible!"

True or false? All contempt
is self-contempt? The photo
of the latest first book prize winner,
big, goofy glasses, toothy, guileless
smile, deliberately stringy hair
& my first thought? "Nice rack!"

Nice rack? I know enough not
to say this out loud. Why don't I
know enough not to think it?

Thin Skin

It's not the drugs, my doctor says,
it's my age. The slightest contact
with something sharp & my skin tears.

I'm bad as a bleeding heart, maybe
worse. I can't finish reading this novel
about Scott & Zelda. When did everything

become so unbearably sad? Remember
when Justin Bieber visited Anne Frank's house?
He wondered out loud, if she lived, would

she be a Belieber? Twenty years ago,
I would have mimed bashing my head
against a wall or biting my hand to keep

from screaming. Now, dressing
today's wound, I settle for a bad pun,
Belieb it or not....

Fuzzy Tree

After bathing in heavy cream,
I turn down the covers
of my Procrustean bed,
"itching" (as the song goes)
"like a man on a fuzzy tree"
who's "gonna need an ocean
of calamine lotion…."
When I asked Google
if climate change could cause
what feels like terminal skin-itch,
resistant so far to every possible
lotion & remedy, my computer
crashed for good. At five a.m.,
finally falling asleep, I wonder
which of my two recurrent bad dreams
I'll experience: stranded
in Whole Foods, traumatized
by the fifty different brands
of organic bone broth or boarding
a city bus whose suicidal driver
has decided today's the day.

Shotgun

The last time I felt good?
Taking out the garbage,
I wobbled against our car,
bumping its side view mirror,
which sagged, sounding
like a broken wind chime.
When I asked the service rep
how much to fix it, with a
straight face, he replied $650.
I bet he'd never before had
an elderly gentleman shout
"Are you fuckin' nuts?"
& lay rubber as he vacated
the premises. I felt good!

My hearing's gone,
my eyesight's going
as if my body wants to say
farewell before I'm ready.
Getting old's a bore. Hearing
or writing about it, even worse.
Ask Hemingway, who ate

his shotgun as if growing old
doesn't beat the alternative.
Sometimes I feel
like a Family Dollar store
in a dying strip mall.
But why dwell on it?

Oh, look! A roadrunner!

Boomer

My grown son, teasing,
thanks me for the anxiety
he inherited. He says, "O.K.,
Boomer" when I refuse to use
the gender-neutral singular "they."

Now he emails, "Hey, Dad, self-explore
your place in the world, read
Me and White Supremacy." WTF?

Didn't I march on Birmingham
with Dr. King? Didn't I triage
those students at Kent State?
Didn't I chain myself to that smokestack
in Alberta? Well, no, I didn't.
But I was there in spirit.

Joking, Randy Newman recalls
Bruce Springsteen telling him, "Rand,
I'm tired. How would you
like to be The Boss for awhile?"

I swear I never told my son, "Ev,
I'm tired of being angry. How would
you like to be angry for awhile?"

The Grilling Dead

Did you hear? A COVID victim
came back to life in a Denver mortuary
& bit several attendants—
a joke posted on Facebook,

but over 70 million Americans
panicked, fortified their homes,
hoarded hazmat suits & assault rifles
& reported their neighbors, who,
grilling peculiar cuts of meat
over cold coals, cried as they ate.

Don't panic, fellow citizens,
Proud Boys & Proud Girls!

Ever hear of Bogorad syndrome?
A condition that causes you to cry
while you're eating, a reflex
of regenerating autonomic fibers, not
zombie guilt over eating the relatives.

Anyway. That's science.
Speaking of which,

to quote the last words
of another dying Anti-vaxxer,
"you do you, I'll do me."

Plague Mask

My wife models the new face mask
she ordered from Amazon, its material
a profusion of extravagant blossoms
that enhance her green-gold irises & the cute
little crease between her eyes. I'm studying
my navel, the skin just above it, hirsute
& blotched, how it pulses to the beat
of my heart. I never understood Newton's
First Law of Motion, but the Fourth Law
of Motion, which I just invented, promises
the heart will always persist in its state
of uniform motion. Let us pray.

New Poems

Here Comes the Sun

The sun rose
at 3 a.m., blistering
what's left
of the succulents
in our garden. When

an apex predator
confronts you,
don't run. Assume
the submissive posture:
bow your head
to protect your throat
& avoid direct eye contact.

Head bowed, eyes
lowered, I slowly
backed away into
some shade.

Yesternow

Hands at ten & two,
late Miles on Bluetooth,

I'm driving north, stopping
again & again

to bury roadkill,
a javelina, jackrabbits,

three diamondbacks, even a
young red-tailed hawk.

I'm driving north, where
I once rode my old gelding

around the reservation,
visiting the hogans

of my friends. We'd
drink coffee & laugh

at my little orange horse,
his cow hocks, his blaze face

& nasty disposition.
Listening to Miles play

"Yesternow," I'm driving north,
yes, where it once rained.

Hav-A-Hart

A year ago, after field mice
infested our gated community,
I checked on the snap traps I'd set
in the guest house the night before.
2 dead mice, one by the door, its head
crushed under the hammer, oozing.
The other dead from exhaustion,
I think, it must have dragged
around all night the trap
snapped onto its tail.

I don't believe in karma
or personifying animals, too
sentimental, describing some mouse
as a political prisoner dragging his ball
& chain until he collapses. I imagine
the suffering of all sentient beings
as a kind of smog rising
into the atmosphere, where it
collects, a heaven of pain.

Miles on Bluetooth messing around
with "Ain't Necessarily So,"

dropping notes, then swinging
into a subtle groove while
from the back seat, Rodney the Roof Rat,
head like a hairy door wedge, rattles
the bars of his Hav-A-Hart cage.

He's a rat, so I'm not sure about
his musical tastes. I do know
if he were human, he'd be relieved
we're driving to the banks
of the Rillito River, where I plan
to release him into 112 degree heat
& an uncertain future.

White Giant

Do stories heal us?
The jury's still out
in the Court of Public Opinion
(whatever that is).

His story? He inherited
a shack in the mountains
& got off the grid, taking his
dog & his parakeet.

Did I get his postcards? No,
just that one letter
about the White Giant flea infestation,
how he emptied 20 canisters
of Morton's salt inside the shack,
then drank a bottle of bourbon
to celebrate the desiccated
flea corpses crackling
underfoot. He came to
on the floor, eye level
with a winter wonderland,
drifts & hillocks of salt.

Back in town, he tells me
he'd contemplated suicide,
too many overheard conversations
about Lizard People,
"you know, Covid vaccines
contain synthetic King Cobra venom,
the Evil One's DNA, which mixes
with your God-created DNA,
making you a hybrid Satan."

He's glad to be back
among those who suspect
"smarter than a pool noodle"
isn't a compliment.

Cat & Apocalypse II

As Roseanne Cash sings,
"This has happened before,"
this image of our little black cat
lapping water from the bathroom sink,
the world outside on fire. Now
she's curled inside the cool porcelain
while I "drain the weasel," an expression
that drives my wife to boycott me
for days, emotionally & sexually,
a high price to pay for what she calls
my middle-school sense of humor.
I'm not laughing. I'm wondering
what our cat will encounter
after the thermonuclear flash-bang,
how she'll survive once she abandons
her porcelain bomb shelter
to become, at last, an outdoor cat.

Family Values

My friend's young Rottweiler
growled at his 5-year-old son.

He drove the dog
into the desert & shot her

in the head. I'm not like him.
He's blue collar, Mexican-

American, a family man,
which may or may not

account for the story & how
he told it, so matter-of-fact.

Staring into my beer, I wondered
if he rolled down the window

to let her smell the scent
of creosote & sage.

The Last Generation

A cliché, comparing rain
to tears. How about something
fresh? A field, no, an arroyo.
It's raining door plugs!

I'm going to dub
the next generation
before the media can,
Generation Trauma or
maybe Generation Last
I'll call them, faced with
feral gangs, wildfire & flood,
weaponized bulldozers,
carcinogenic air & necrotic soil.

An 80-year-old wrote
a letter to the editor
apologizing to future generations
for the toxic waste dump
they'll inherit. WTF?
Making amends, Step 8 of H.A.,
the Humans Anonymous program?
Officious asshole.

I rode a bike to work
for thirty years. I helped monkey-wrench
Big Oil. I even sneaked around
at night, super-gluing "I Pollute"
bumper stickers onto the neighbors'
Humvees & SUVs. To paraphrase a line
from "Roll Away The Stone,"
that old Nitty Gritty Dirt Band song,

"I was good, but I could have been
better." Like most of us.
Gen Last, no need to forgive me
for this open sewer we call home.

The Spirit Animal Society

Every five years,
the Spirit Animal Society
mandates its members
rigorously interrogate
their own personal growth,
selecting a new spirit animal
if appropriate. My new one?

The koala, not because it's
cute & cuddly (which it is
& I'm not) but because it
sleeps 23 hours a day, both
inspiring me & relieving
my guilt about wasting
my post post-salad days.

I slept 21 hours again,
no bedsores yet, my life coach,
short & stout, whispering
in my drowsy ear, don't
worry, baby, we'll wake you up
if you're ever needed.

Viejo

She
dressed me
with her eyes.

Help! I've Fallen....

My daughter-in-law, the sleep specialist,
knows I'm non-compliant. I read in bed.
I take long naps every afternoon, the cat
tucked, purring against my neck, drooling,
his cheek against mine. Late evening, I sit
at the computer, handicapping tomorrow's races
or watching porn until the "acting"
bores me. Old guys just wanna have fun.

Of course, I can't sleep. At 2 a.m., my eyes
aching, I chew a gummy. At 3, dizzy,
not stoned or high, I need to pee again
& I hoist myself off the sofa, grabbing
an end table, the arm of a chair, the cat tower,
wobbling down the hall. I imagine calling
from the bathroom floor, panic disguised
as humor, "Help! I've fallen & I can't
get up," hoping I'll still recognize
whoever comes to rescue me.

80 Is the New 50

80, the new 50?
Tell that to my right hip.

Don't bullshit me
until you've limped a mile
in my body. If aging

is "a natural & beneficial
part of life," why
flinch when someone
asks your age?

Full-grown Human On Board
double-clutches past the entrance
to *Funeraria del Angel.*

Hermit

I haven't left the house in weeks,
limping room to room, forgetting
what I came for, wearing unwashed
the goose-turd green flannel pajamas
I inherited from my mother-in-law's awful
second husband. On Netflix last night,
a precociously ironic five-year-old
protested, "Of course, I love popcorn!
I'm not an animal!" Then again,
I myself might be an animal, one
of the dumber ones unfazed by guilt,
that useless emotion, arranging
& re-arranging the bottles of hand lotion
you left behind & imagining I'm
now living inside my favorite meme,
a hermit's cave, a sign scrawled
above the entrance, "free hugs!"

Microwave

When my wife calls me
from the other room, I crawl
under my desk & hide, my feet
visible, a serious joke that
always makes her laugh.
She chuckles, then asks what
I did with our old microwave.
"Nothing," I reply. "I left it
at the curb." "It's gone," she says
& we exchange fist-bumps, beaming
as if our on-its-last-legs appliance
will transform someone's life,
someone like the homeless guy
on the median who touched my fingers
as I gave him some spare change.
Speeding away, I groped
inside the glove compartment
for the hand sanitizer. What was I
supposed to do? Invite him home
for a soak in our hot tub? Such a drag,
liberal guilt. I imagine the scum
foaming brown as Guinness
on the surface of the water
after he leaves. I can imagine
draining the hot tub, scrubbing it,

then picking up the towel he used,
his beard & torso faintly outlined
on the damp terry cloth. I don't know
whether to post the image as a serious joke
on the Shroud of Turin webpage, which
proclaims the artifact verification
of "God's reckless love"

or just throw the dirty towel in the wash.

Business as Usual

Whenever I see the word "gritty"
in a blurb, I think "grit"

as in dirt or "gristy" as in "grist
for one's mill." Then I think

of the signage I was once hired
to sell: "Sorry, We're Open" placards
no business wanted to buy.

My definition of "entrepreneur"?
"Greedy opportunist" though Google
& the Chamber of Commerce disagree.

Let's give it up for the creative who
coined the phrase "the deserving rich."

Body Poetry

Every blurb I read these days
belabors the word "body"

as if Western Civ's obsession
with the soul never mattered,

as if we're all dying to read poetry
about "the sodomized city of their body."

The female body, the Black
body, the queer & trans body,

body this & body that,
as if the colonizing gaze

has reduced us all
to an underground army
of life-like terra-cotta figures.

American Chestnut

The soldiers woke us at 5 a.m.,
a bullhorn announcing we had
an hour to pack our belongings
& leave. 200 years we've lived
in this glade, subsisting on cow's milk
& white rice, Sundays, sittin'
on the porch, pickin' & a-grinnin'
as the old song says. I left a note
for those who will replace us:
God damn you all! (& please
fertilize twice a year the chestnut tree
out back, the last of its kind.)

Kufi

You call my Kenyan kufi
"cultural appropriation."
I call it "cultural appreciation"
& cock it over one eye.

You spurn as "anthropocentric"
the field guide's translation
of a white-winged dove's call
as "who-cooks-for-you?"

"Who cooks for you?"
the doves asked all afternoon.

Remember when you were little,
the musical trout I bought you,
flapping on its plaque
& singing "bad to the bone"?
You laughed so hard,
oatmeal came out your nose.

Dear son, I bequeath to you
whatever's left of my humorless
& youthful certainty. Enjoy.

Sugar, Sugar

When I grab my wife & growl
"Give me some sugar!"
she giggles & breaks out
of my embrace, certain I'm
just foolin'. I'm not. As Blake
may have said, "You never know
how much sugar is enough
unless you know what's
more than enough."
My son asks his toddler
what she wants for dinner.
Just foolin', I suggest a handful
of lollipops. My boy presses
a forefinger to his lips, glaring at me
as if I've said something wrong.

What Is Porn?

Five feet of heaven
& no body hair,
a callow boy snatching
back his hands,
his step-sister's proffered breasts
like hot plates, then
the inevitable mood change
from badly-acted dismay
to badly-acted lust.

My definition? Unsure,
I asked around, aware,
for Millennials, pornography's
just another vocation.
My very own Millennial
protested the word
"licentious" in my definition
though, because he's
a good boy, he asked me
how to pronounce it.

The Pope

When asked what famous person
I'd choose to have dinner with,
I always reply John XII,
Supreme Pontiff from 955–964 AD.

Gibbon describes him thus:
"he lived in public adultery
with the matrons of Rome,
the lateran palace a school
of prostitution, his rapes
of virgins and widows
deterred female pilgrims
from visiting the tomb of St. Peter,
lest in the devout act they should be
violated by his successor."

I'd ask my sister the therapist
to join us for salads at Subway.
In her high-school Italian,
she'd ask him tactful questions
as he sat there, small as a child,
his red-slippered feet not
touching the floor, eyeing
every woman jogging
past the window.

I'd simply watch him eat—
rapist, castrator, alleged
murderer, this creature so alien
to our plant-based souls—
I'd watch & wonder what's
the Latin word for "why?"

High Hopes

"No, I don't like that,"
says my granddaughter,
two-years-old and already
dealing with the world.
She also knows "That's mine!"
& "Wake up, Grandpa!"

My prettiest sister's shrine
to our late father featured
a framed portrait of his look-alike,
Charlton Heston, darling
of the NRA. But I've got

high hopes—just the other day,
I tickled my granddaughter
& she pushed my hand away,
glaring & said "No means no!"

They Told Me to Interrogate My White Male Cishet Privilege

Purring in my lap,
our little black cat, suddenly

overcome, nips me in the armpit,
a love-bite that disrupts

this morning's prayer:
"O Lord, make of my enemies

footstools. If you're busy,
I understand." Interrogate

myself? What, the old
bad cop/bad cop routine?

Meditating

Cross-legged,
facing east, sometimes
west, sometimes north
or south, which also works,
meaning finally facing
inward, where
we've been told
bliss awaits.
Not so sure
though I'm learning
to accept goal-less goals,
meatless meat,
but loveless love?
No, no way.

About the Author

Jefferson Carter has work in such journals as *Carolina Quarterly*, *Barrow Street*, and *Rattle*. Chax Press published his ninth collection, *Get Serious: New and Selected Poems*, a Southwest Best Book of 2013. *Yesternow*, his twelfth book, is available through his website: jeffersoncarterverse.com.

Carter lives in Tucson with his wife Connie. He taught composition and poetry for 30 years at Pima Community College.

Current Coyote Arts Titles

Gilbert Alter-Gilbert, editor. *Pipe Dreams: The Drug Experience in Literature*
Jefferson Carter. *Free Hugs: New and Selected Poems*
Joe Martin. *Rumi's Mathnavi: A Theatre Adaptation*
Lawrence Millman. *Goodbye, Ice: Arctic Poems*
Lawrence Millman. *Outsider: My Boyhood with Thoreau* (illustrated by Geoff Halverson)
Elias Papadimitrakopoulos. *Toothpaste with Chlorophyll | Maritime Hot Baths* (translated from the Greek by John Taylor; illustrated by Alekos Fassianos)
Eric Paul Shaffer. *A Million-Dollar Bill: Poems*
Eric Paul Shaffer. *Free Speech: Poems*
Eric Paul Shaffer. *Green Leaves: Selected & New Poems*
Christopher Spranger. *The Book of Tasks, Volume I: Atlantean Undertakings*
Christopher Spranger. *The Comedy of Agony: A Book of Poisonous Contemplations*
Leslie Stahlhut. *The Secret of the Old Cloche: Agatha Christine Mystery Stories*
John Taylor. *What Comes from the Night: Poems*

Forthcoming Coyote Arts Titles

Eric Basso. *Fictions: The Beak Doctor: Short Fictions, 1972–1976 & Bartholomew Fair*
Greg Boyd. *Brotherton's Travels: Memoirs*
René Daumal. *The Anti-Heaven*
  (translated and with an introduction by Jordan Jones)
Kendall Lappin. *Dead French Poets Speak Plain English & Memoirs of a Translator of Poetry*
Joe Martin. *Parabola: Shorter Fictions*
Gérard de Nerval. *Aurélia, followed by Sylvie*
  (translated by Kendall Lappin and with an introduction by Eric Basso)
Eric Paul Shaffer. *Second Nature: Poems*
Leslie Stahlhut. *Borderlands of the Heart and Other Stories*
Leslie Stahlhut. *The Hidden Staircase: Agatha Christine Mystery Stories, #2*